MALAYSIA

PORTRAIT OF A NATION

Photography by Radin Mohd Noh Saleh

Text by Wendy Khadijah Moore

PERIPLUS

Published by Periplus Editions
with editorial offices at 130 Joo Seng Road #06-01/03, Singapore 368357

Copyright © 2003 Periplus Editions (HK) Ltd
ALL RIGHTS RESERVED
ISBN 962-593-989-X
Printed in Singapore

All photographs by Radin Mohd Noh Saleh except the following:
pp. 12 (bottom left), 51 (left & right) by Tommy Chang; pp. 13 (bottom left), 28 (top middle & bottom right), 29, 32 (top & bottom), 34 (top), 35, 49 (top right & bottom middle), 51 (middle), 78, 94 by Jill Gocher; pp. 23 (top right), 24, 28 (bottom middle), 45 (top & bottom), 46 (right), 76 (right), 80, 81, 82, 84 (bottom), 88, 88–89 by Ravi John Smith; pp. 9, 10 (bottom), 12 (top left & right), 13 (top left); 23 (bottom right), 32–33, 40, 42 (top left), 46 (middle), 47, 67, 73, 75, 76 (left), 84 (top), 85, 86 by Arthur Teng; pp. 92, 93 (all) by Jacob Termansen; front & back endpapers, pp. 4, 8, 20 (top), 21, 23 (bottom left), 26, 27, 28 (bottom left), 30, 31, 36, 37, 48, 49 (top middle & bottom left), 52, 53, 56 (all), 64 (all); 72–73, 87 (top), 90, 91 (all) by Luca Tettoni Photography; p. 74 by Ariel Tunguia.

Distributors

North America, Latin America and Europe Tuttle Publishing
364 Innovation Drive, North Clarendon, VT 05759-9436, USA
Tel: (802) 773 8930, Fax: (802) 526 6993, E-mail: info@tuttlepublishing.com

Asia Pacific Berkeley Books Pte Ltd
130 Joo Seng Road #06-01/03, Singapore 368357
Tel: (65) 6280 3320, Fax: (65) 6280 6290, E-mail: inquiries@periplus.com.sg

Japan and Korea Tuttle Publishing
Yaekari Building, 3F, 5-4-12 Osaki, Shinagawa-ku, Tokyo 141-0032
Tel: (813) 5437 6171, Fax: (813) 5437 0755, E-mail: tuttle-sales@gol.com

Front endpaper: Every design has a symbolic meaning in handwoven Iban textiles, known as *pua kumbu*.
Back endpaper: Silk brocades, known as *songket*, are the speciality of Malay weavers.
Right: This shadow puppet figure, Siti Dewi, is made from cowhide or goatskin, hence the name *wayang kulit* ("skin or leather theatre").
Opposite: Spectacular sunsets staged on an island-studded horizon is one of the reasons Pulau Langkawi's Pantai Tengah is such a famous resort beach.

CONTENTS

THE LAND WHERE THE WINDS MEET

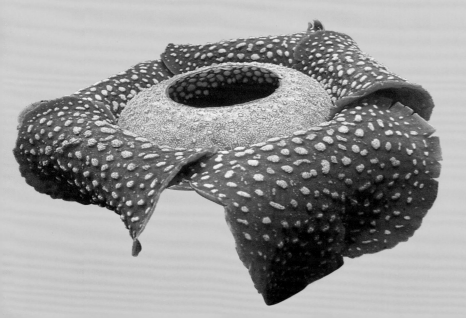

Some places are not what they seem. Like people, some are easy to get to know, their personalities on show for all to see, and once known they remain constant, caught in a kind of timelessness. Others are more difficult to penetrate, not only in their geography but also in their psyche. At first you think you know them, but then they change again, chameleon-like, and by degrees they become stranger. For me, Malaysia is this kind of place. It has been like this ever since my first visit over three decades ago. It is a country that offers almost unparalleled diversity, from it geographical contrasts to its kaleidoscopic population. Here is travel in variety and depth of feeling.

Immersed in Kuala Lumpur's *Blade Runner*-like cityscape, I can marvel at the world's tallest buildings, but also spy the world's oldest rainforests in the hills beyond. I can cruise the superhighways and be numbed by the banality of concrete suburbia, then take an exit and emerge in an idyllic Gauguinesque village. I can spend the morning mall-crawling through designer boutiques and the afternoon exploring the crowded lanes of ancient port cities, or I can even escape to a tropical island and play "Survivor" or join the lotus eaters at some of this planet's most exclusive resorts.

Malaysia is an old land, but an imagined nation, inheriting its political borders from the imperialist powers that carved up the great Malay World into Dutch and English spheres. The Malay Peninsula, formerly Malaya, dangles like an appendage from Asia's southeastern extremity, while across the South China Sea are the states of Sabah and Sarawak on the great jungled island of Borneo. Combined, the nation they create is home to a diverse population of almost 24 million, with a geography that is equally varied. It offers a journey through both space and time. It is a nation that exists in the past and present in a kind of duality – a balancing act that is at the heart of understanding the paradox that is Malaysia. Let me explain.

There are two windows in my hotel room in Kota Bharu, the far-flung capital of the Malay heartland, Kelantan. One overlooks the roofs of wooden houses, just discernible through the verdant overhang of mango trees and coconut palms. From here come the sounds of cockerels' cries and the "tock-tock" of stone pestles against mortars, grinding spices. Reassured by the past, I open the other window, where instantly I am confronted with the face of the future. The drone of air-conditioners floats across

Previous page, left: Measuring up to a metre in width, the world's largest flower, the parasitic, leafless rafflesia, is found only in the rainforests of Borneo and Sumatra at altitudes of 500 to 700 metres.
Previous page, right: Kuala Lumpur's skyline is dominated by the 451.9-metre-high Petronas Twin Towers, among the world's tallest buildings, designed by Cesar Pelli and built between 1993 and 1996.
Left: At Penang's tourist mecca of Batu Ferringhi, beachgoers don't have to walk far to buy a locally made batik sarong.
Right, top: At Kuala Muda, in the south of the rice-bowl state of Kedah, kampong houses are set high on posts amidst tall coconut palms.
Right, bottom: At Bachok, in Kelantan, fishermen still put to sea in wooden praus that are launched from the beach.

a tarred parking lot where Mercedes Benzes and locally made Protons stand in gleaming ranks where not so long ago a village stood. Malaysia is like the hotel room, a limbo land, albeit a comfortable one, where you exist somewhere between the past and the present – the divide between traditional and contemporary.

It is not a new concept though. Malaysia has always been adept at re-creation, and its undeniable success has been to constantly absorb change while somehow staying the same. Geography has played a major role. At the heart of Southeast Asia, straddling the ancient trade routes where the monsoon winds meet, this land has attracted visitors for thousands of years, bringing with them their cultures, languages and religions.

This is the changing face of Malaysia. At the same time, there is the constant of that which has always been.

This dualism has long been known, beautifully expressed by the ancient Malay saying, "*adat* (tradition) comes from the mountains and religion from the sea". The mountains, home to the world's oldest rainforests, are a wonderful metaphor for the past. Here live the remnant tribes of Orang Asli, "the original people". Here shamans still go to acquire their knowledge from fairy princesses. Despite the shrinking of the vast forests, they harbour an astonishing menagerie and a bewildering flora that is still being discovered even as it is being lost. The dense green heart is the source of the mystery that has long fascinated travellers, and it continues to exert a powerful effect on the national psyche.

Six-lane highways cleave mountain ranges shrouded in forests, but few people venture into the rainforest – they drive through it, cocooned in air-conditioned comfort. Yet folk memories remain. They search for the wayside stall that sells jungle durians, renowned for that subtle, mysterious taste that the orchards can never duplicate. Traditionalists who go in search of herbal remedies, or woods for crafts, still chant special mantras to the guardian spirits before entering that other, older world.

Change always came from the sea. The Malays came in their praus, and the rise and fall of their great kingdoms, from Kedah to Melaka, waxed and waned with the seaborne trade. The Indian, Chinese and Arab traders brought their religions and their traditions, although these were never a threat to Islam. The seas brought the colonial powers – the Portuguese, Dutch and English – whose surviving cultural fragments added to the exotic mosaic that is Malaysian culture and history.

Below: Kite makers still practice their craft in Kelantan, where traditional pastimes such as kite flying continue to be popular. **Opposite:** With traditions fast disappearing on the west coast, stage-managed events such as the "Colours of Malaysia" festival, held at Kuala Lumpur's Merdeka Square, is a highlight of the tourism calendar.

Dualism is often present in everyday life. Malaysians have a knack of incorporating both old and new into their lifestyles. Along the Kelantan coast, motors have replaced sails in wooden fishing boats., the old carved spar holders are now kept merely for show, and the symbolism behind the carvings and colours has been forgotten. A world away, in the luxury homes of the capital, conversation can easily swing from the fluctuations of the stock exchange and the horsepower of the latest BMW, to talk of an amorous politician who wooed his new wife with a love potion of jungle herbs, or how the fortunes of a well-known company have soared since a pair of guardian lions were installed in its high-rise office in line with *feng shui* precepts.

Back at the Kota Bharu hotel, as I watch from the hotel window, a dozen families walk to their vehicles, all emblazoned with stickers saying "Mystery Drive", and take off. It seemed almost uncanny that I, too, was there in search of mystery. Only our methods were different – they were on an organized, motorized treasure hunt, while I was on a personal journey – but we were all in our own way looking for clues.

Left, top: Climbers approach the top of Mount Kinabalu, Malaysia's highest peak at 4,101 metres, that dominates the landscape of Sabah.
Left, bottom: Golfers enjoy a game at Tanjung Aru in Sabah.
Right: Kelantan's estuaries are home to Malaysia's most colourful fishing fleet, known as *bangau* boats after their unique carved and painted "stork"-shaped spar holders of the same name.
Following pages, clockwise from top left: Indian garlands for sale in Johor Bahru; a woman puts out salted squid to dry in the sun at Marang in Terengganu; ritual prayers are performed in a Penang temple; an elderly Chinese attendant sells joss sticks at Penang's Snake Temple; women harvest rice by hand in a Melakan rice field; an Indian fortune teller operates from a Penang pavement; women traders dominate at Kota Bharu's colourful Central Market; and a Bajau horseman participates in an annual parade in Kota Belud, Sabah.

"For the fort was the pride of Malacca and after its destruction the place lost its glory, like a woman bereaved of her husband, the lustre gone from her face. But now by the will of Allah it was no more, showing how ephemeral are the things of this world. The old order is destroyed, a new world is created and all around us is change."

— Abdullah bin Adbul Kadir, *Hikayat Abdullah* (1849)

A STEP BACK IN TIME

Upstream from the ancient trading port, inside an old wooden palace where the light filters through carved arabesques, a prince entertains his visitors, a nobleman and a foreigner, with tales befitting the occasion — of court intrigues, patricide, a princess cast under a spell, priceless cloths of gold, black slaves bought in Mecca, and a sultan with dozens of wives.

It evokes a scene from a far-off time, like those depicted in courtly annals when the lands and the seas of the Malay World were controlled by the sultanates, before the Europeans came with their cultural imperialism and everything changed forever. It was all lost, this royal way of life, those feudal kingdoms — or so we were led to believe.

But the event described is not of some long ago time. It is of the here and now. The prince is Tengku Ismail bin Tengku Su, Tengku Ismail for short. The old wooden palace is his home, "Pura Tanjung Sabtu", upriver from the old trading port of Kuala Terengganu. The foreigner is me, the author, while the nobleman is my husband, this book's photographer, whose royal roots go back to Jambi in Sumatra. His family is part of the Malay diaspora that resulted from the colonial invasions, but that is another story.

By contrast, Tengku Ismail was fortunate to experience an upbringing in the traditional royal style, pampered by black slaves, family retainers and household poets who lulled him to sleep in the royal compound. Needless to say, this unique childhood affected his later passions, reviving Terengganu's handwoven silks and restoring old wooden palaces.

History is all around him as every painting and photograph on the walls has a story to tell. There is his great uncle, Sultan Muhammad II, who had 36 wives. There is the princess whose recent untimely death was rumoured to be due to an enemy's spell, and there is the prince who was murdered by his son who had joined a fanatical religious cult.

Malaysia's history is like Tengku Ismail's walls, a glorious mélange of past and present, of royal courts, of vanished kingdoms, of famous battles won and lost, of shamans and spirits, of religions waxing and waning like the tides. Over the centuries, the layers build up, while others erode away, until the present takes form like an old lime-washed wall, exposed to the elements, where the different hues of past owners are revealed like an abstract of the past.

Climate invariably affects history. Its affect in Malaysia is particularly profound, often annihilating the past. The equatorial combination of heat, humidity and torrential rains has not only weathered walls but has, in most cases, wiped out all traces of ancient settlements. Not everywhere though. Away from the ravages of the elements, inside limestone caves, archaeologists have been assembling the jigsaw of Malaysia's earliest days. It is an exercise that is fraught with physical difficulties as well as being a theoretical minefield. Old theories are dismissed in the light of new evidence, as are established dates, with new dating techniques turning the clock back even further into prehistory.

Habitation was once believed to have begun in Borneo with the unearthing of a 40,000-year-old skull in Sarawak's Niah Caves. Now that date is uncertain. Peninsular Malaysia was once thought to be inhabited later, but that theory has been overturned with the discovery of the Kota Tampan stone tool workshop in Perak. Its Pompeii-like demise was linked to the eruption of Sumatra's Lake Toba, said to be 34,000 years ago, but radiocarbon dating may now shift that date back to 100,000 years ago. Strangely, but rather in character with Malaysia's dual persona, the past becomes older the more we move into the future.

Previous page, left: Stone Buddha image, 10th–11th century, found in Kedah's Bujang Valley.
Previous page, right: Travelling artist James Wathen's view of Kedah and Georgetown in 1811.
Opposite: Auguste Nicholas Vaillant's view of Melaka's Town Square with its 18th-century Dutch-built Christ Church and 17th-century Stadthuys.
Below: James Wathen's 1811 view of Porta de Santiago, the last remaining gate of Melaka's Portuguese fortress, A Famosa.

Despite climatic drawbacks, Malaysia pioneered regional archaeology. It all began around 160 years ago when Colonel James Low, on one of his numerous jungle excursions, suddenly discovered "undoubted relics of a Hindoo Colony, with ruins of temples". Little did he know then that he had stumbled upon Malaysia's richest archaeological region, now known as the Bujang Valley, and that his discovery would pave the way for later archaeologists to solve one of Southeast Asia's most intriguing historical puzzles – the location of the legendary kingdom of Kedah that flourished from the 5th to the 14th century.

Low's theory of a Hindu colony has long been relegated to the dustbins of history. Kedah was more likely a long-standing Malay trading kingdom which had incorporated Indian cultural elements into its lifestyle, beginning with Buddhist and then later Hindu influences. But the religion that would have the greatest effect on Malaysia, and provide the impetus for its greatest kingdom – Melaka – was Islam.

Melaka is to Malaysia what Athens is to Greece. Even though its fame was brief, lasting a little over a century before the Portuguese conquered it in 1511, its effect on the psyche of Malaysia, its culture, attitudes, fashions, royal houses, language and literature are still being felt over six centuries later.

In Melaka, and in the sultanates it spawned, rulers enjoyed absolute power. The concept of *daulat*, a type of mystical kingly power, placed the sultan above society and criticism. However,

Top: The residence of Dato Klana, the Malay chieftain of Sungai Ujong, near Seremban, in the 1870s.
Bottom: In inland areas, elephants were the major means of transport in Perak until the early 20th century.

tales abound of rulers who failed because they did not heed their ministers' advice. The feudal days are long gone, but the sultanates remain, although their powers were curtailed by colonial laws and eroded further in recent times.

Like the rings of a tree, history is layered. Throughout Malaysia, these tiers are visible in some places more than others, especially in Melaka. Here, the incursions of Malays, Portuguese, Dutch, English, and the Malays again, are interspersed with influxes of Chinese, Indians, Arabs, Javanese, Bugis, and scores more. A glance at a map can show why Melaka was such a successful trading kingdom. The southeast trade winds blew dhows and caravels across the Indian Ocean, the northeast monsoon delivered the junks and praus from the South China Sea and the Malay Archipelago, and all of them were funnelled through the channel that came to be known as the Strait of Melaka.

The Peninsula's strategic location was also its undoing. Although the Portuguese and the Dutch only ever held Melaka, the next interlopers, the English, were stunningly successful. Penang, their first base, was acquired by trickery in 1786 from the Sultan of Kedah. Singapore was then established, in 1819. Melaka was a "gift" from the Dutch when the British and the Hollanders carved up the Malay World into their own spheres in 1824, and from these Straits Settlements they gradually planted British Residents in the Peninsular states. Even Borneo was not spared. In 1848, James Brooke became Rajah of Sarawak

Right: These noblewomen from the royal court of Perak, photographed in the early 20th century, are wearing the typical Malay costume of the time: a long, loose blouse fastened down the front with jewelled pins, a handwoven checked sarong, and a sumptuous silk *songket* shawl.

by quelling a rebellion against the Brunei court, while Sabah ultimately came under the "ownership" of British merchants. But it was not all smooth going. Malay rebellions had to be quelled in Perak, Pahang, Negeri Sembilan and Sabah, and under the guise of anti-piracy campaigns Brooke emasculated Sarawak's Iban and other tribes. Johor held out longer than the other western states, and there was anger when Siam ceded Kelantan, Terengganu and Kedah to the British. By 1919, however, the Union Jack fluttered over all: British Malaya was complete.

The colonial masters perpetuated the myth that Malaya belonged to the Malays, but the reality was different. Resentment was already simmering when World War II and the Japanese Occupation put paid to the might of the British Empire. Independence was already an issue when the British took up the tenuous reins again after the war, but plans were put on hold following the outbreak of the Malayan Emergency, when disenchanted Chinese swelled the ranks of the communist guerrillas who embarked on a terror campaign against the British. Finally, in 1957, Britain relinquished its sovereignty, and the first Prime Minister, Tunku Abdul Rahman, declared Malaya independent. Six years later, Singapore, Sabah and Sarawak joined with Malaya to form Malaysia, but in 1965 Singapore broke away to become a separate nation.

Top: Kuching's High Court, built in 1874, is one of Malaysia's finest surviving Georgian-style buildings.
Bottom: Established by the second White Rajah of Sarawak, Charles Brooke, in 1891, the renowned Sarawak Museum houses a fascinating display of Sarawak's enthnography, natural history and antique jars.
Right: Fort Margherita, named after Rajah Charles' wife Margaret, was completed in 1879. It is now a Police Museum, with displays ranging from blunderbusses and pirates' swords to brass cannon and early gallows.

The British legacy provided a ready-made administration, schools, roads, railways, a judicial system, plantations and tin mines, but the bugbear was the fractured cultural polity, the result of large immigrant intakes from China and India, and the successful colonial policy of "divide and rule". As a result, ethnic disturbances in 1969 saw the introduction of policies designed for a more equitable distribution of wealth.

Boom time came in the mid-1980s, and for well over a decade the economy grew meteorically. Under the motto "Malaysia boleh" (Malaysia can do it), everything seemed possible. The world's tallest buildings, the futuristic IT community, the region's largest airport, huge dams, and land reclamations were all underway when, in 1997, the bottom fell out of Asia's boom. Overnight the ringgit plunged, the stock market crashed, and construction sites became ghost towns.

But one thing that Malaysia is always good at is reinvention. In the wake of the economic crisis, new multiethnic political parties emerged that signal a move away from the ethnic-based parties of the past. However, the old warning from the Melakan sultanate, that urges leaders to listen to their ministers, is still, like much of the lessons of the past, relevant in today's Malaysia.

Left: The predominantly red-tiled roofs and narrow streets of Melaka's Chinatown can be viewed from the minaret of Masjid Kampung Kling, the town's earliest mosque, built in 1748.
Right, clockwise from top left: Istana Kenangan, in the royal town of Kuala Kangsar, Perak, is renowned for its intricate woven and painted wall panels and fine filagree carvings; decorative, century-old townhouses of the Straits Chinese line Jonkers Street in Melaka; the Muzium Budaya (Cultural Museum) at Melaka was built to the specifications of the 15th-century palace of Sultan Mahmud Shah, as described in the *Sejarah Melayu* (Malay Annals); Kuala Kangsar's Ubudiah Mosque, built by the British administration in 1913–17, displays distinctive Mogul influences.

"In time the marvels of the natural scenery pall upon the sight, the jungle riots too much in the vision, which despairs of ever forming for the mind a connected picture to take away. But the Malays have given the country the only beauties in it provided by the hand of man. Touching this responsive land they have adorned it, and still continue to adorn, and whether you live here or merely flash through, yet the pictures the Malays have provided are carried in your brain."

— Cuthbert Woodville Harrison, *Illustrated Guide to the Federated Malay States* (1923)

RICHES OF THE TROPICAL RAINFOREST

There was a set formula in the 19th century for Penang's early ecotourists: a ride from Georgetown in a horse-drawn cart to the Botanic Gardens, a refreshing bath amid the towering jungle at the famed waterfall – the gardens are also called the Waterfall Gardens – and then a ride by Sumatran pony, or by a sedan car (for women) carried by coolies, up the winding trail to the hill station. Once at the top, invigorated by the cooler climate, the visitors took walks – a pursuit considered too enervating in the lowlands – and marvelled at the juxtaposition of the tamed and the untamed, where tropical and temperate blooms thrived in the immaculate gardens, backed by the luxuriant botanical marvels of the virgin rainforests.

Now, at the beginning of the 21st century, the formula and the transport have changed, but the trails, the waterfall, the gardens (with their plethora of aggressive macaques) and the hill station still exist, as does the uniquely Malaysian concept, noted by those early travellers, of the juxtaposition between the tamed and the untamed. Oddly enough, although the forests have dwindled, time has not altered this divide. The change is still acute.

On Penang Hill, I wander past the old colonial retreats, with names like "Browhead" and "Fernhill", belying their original owners' origins, with their carefully tended lawns, topiary and flower gardens, and then, abruptly, the resort ends and the forest begins.

Serried rows of tree trunks, bare of branches for perhaps 20 metres, shoot skywards to where their leafy canopies conceal the sky. Where the light does manage to penetrate — like sunrays through skylights in Gothic cathedrals — bamboos and ferns proliferate, fighting each other for space. Strangler figs and lianas drape the towering trees like rigging on ghostly galleons, and lichens and epiphytes ornament and decorate their limbs. It is beautiful in that wild, untamed way, and its mystery has by no means decreased with time. Despite the popularity of four-wheel-drive clubs, nature societies and wilderness adventure, for many Malaysians the *hutan* (jungle) still personifies the unknown — the realm where spirits dwell, a primitive, dark, uncomfortable place — that is forever juxtaposed against the sunny, open coastlines and river banks. The known and the unknown, the primitive and the civilized, the dark and the light — that is the paradox. "We freed ourselves," exclaimed a writer emerging from the rainforest into the cleared land, and perhaps it is a sense of this in a long-forgotten communal memory that seals the divide.

Previous page, left: The hibiscus, or *bunga raya*, is Malaysia's national flower and is widely grown throughout the country.
Previous page, right: Bird's-nest ferns, tree ferns and palms proliferate in the rainforests of Cameron Highlands where cooler temperatures make trekking a delight.
Left: A two-storey longhouse of the Orang Ulu is recreated under the forested flank of Mount Santubong at the Sarawak Cultural Village, set on a 6-hectare site on the coast north of Kuching.

Many Malaysians still believe that the forest is a source of power. Traditional healers acquire their knowledge in its depths, and many jungle cures, like the potent virility-giving root *tongkat ali*, as well as a host of other herbal remedies, are more popular than ever before. There are other clues, too. Sometimes one can spot a lone forest giant in the midst of an oil palm plantation, or on the outskirts of a town, left by those who cleared the land to house the dislocated spirits. In the grounds of a five-star resort in Terengganu, I spied a nail hammered in an old tree, a popular way to kill the spirit of a *pontianak*, the ghost of a woman who died in childbirth. Even on Sabah's Mount Kinabalu, the venue of the world's "toughest mountain race" and the goal of thousands of climbers each year, chickens are still sacrificed in an annual ritual to appease the mountain's guardians.

Only a century ago, virgin rainforests stretched from one coast to the other, both in Peninsular Malaysia and the Bornean states of Sabah and Sarawak. A *terra incognita*, the Victorian traveller Isabella Bird called it in 1879, "a vast and malarious equatorial jungle sparsely populated", while her contemporary, Hugh Clifford, likened it to the Sphinx: "She propounds riddles few can answer, luring us onward with illusive hopes of inspiring revelations, yet hiding … the secrets of the oldest and least amply recorded of human histories."

Today, over half of Malaysia is still forested, a figure that the government maintains it will preserve, but the enormous land clearing for oil palm and rubber plantations in the past,

Right: Sabah provides some of the world's best diving, especially on the east coast of Sabah where Pulau Sipadan, Malaysia's only oceanic island, has a 600-metre drop-off and a dazzling array of tropical fish and corals.

Above, clockwise from top left: Amongst the bewildering variety of Malaysian plants, both indigenous and exotic, is the flower of the cannonball tree found in Penang's Botanic Gardens; the carnivorous pitcher plant from the Mulu National Park in Sarawak; the brilliantly coloured ginger plant that adorns the forests at Fraser's Hill; the pineapple-shaped fruit of the coastal pandanus; delicate spider orchids, one Malaysia's hundreds of species; and pale pink new leaves on a hardwood tree.

combined with overlogging and some disastrous forest fires have seen the share of virgin forest shrink dramatically, and with it the loss of animal habitats. Some states though, like Sabah, are seriously addressing the problem, and with an ever-increasing list of protected areas and nature parks, including Kinabalu Park, Malaysia's first World Heritage Site, it is leading the way for other states to follow.

Despite their decreasing acreage, the great rainforests still cover vast tracts. One of the most impressive is Taman Negara, Peninsular Malaysia's original national park, set up in 1939 after an exhaustive enquiry into animal numbers when colonial officials travelled the length and breadth of the country questioning local people. The results make fascinating, but sometimes depressing, reading. Old-timers remembered large herds of elephants, rhinoceros and seladang (wild oxen) in the Perak coastal forests, now almost all cleared for plantations and agriculture, but even in the 1930s numbers had dwindled. Many farmers then viewed big game as a menace, but one enlightened headman in Jelebu, Negeri Sembilan, had this to say: "The rich should not hurt the poor, the great should not harm the humble, nor should men oppress the animals of the jungle."

Although the country lacks great spectacles of large herds of animals, since it lacks open plains, it more than makes up for this by having one of the richest, most complex and diverse arrays of flora and fauna on earth. The forests of Sabah and Sarawak, in particular, are host to the bizarre as well as the beautiful, among

Right: At Sarawak's Semonggok wildlife rehabilitation centre, 20 kilometres south of Kuching, orang-utan that were once kept as illegal pets, are taught forest skills before being released into the wild.

them the remarkable parasitic rafflesia which manifests itself as a massive flower; the cup-like pitcher plant which traps water and insects alike; over 3,000 species of orchid in an enormous range of shapes and colours; the long-nosed, pot-bellied proboscis monkey; the shy and cryptic orang-utan; the handsome sun bear; and the spectacular hornbill.

Most Malaysians, however, as well as most travellers, opt for the tamed environment, viewing the untamed realms from the comfortable confines of a car, train, boat or plane. Even in the old days, apart from the forest-dwelling Orang Asli and Penan, the bulk of the population lived, as it does now, on the fertile lowlands along the coasts and the river banks. Just as Penang's early travellers noticed the startling contrast of the rainforests to the hill station gardens, this same wild backdrop also provides a stunning counterpoint to the emerald green rice fields, manicured tea estates, fishing villages, palm-clad beaches and tropical islands that Malaysia is also famed for.

Malaysia's total land area is almost 132,000 square kilometres, of which well over half comprise the Bornean states of Sabah and Sarawak. Of the oft-quoted 75 per cent forest cover throughout the country, at least 25 per cent of this comprises rubber and oil palm plantations, which cover large tracts of former lowland rainforests in all states. In Kedah and Kelantan, the fertile river plains have long been the nation's rice bowl.

Left: The largest island off the east coast of Peninsular Malaysia, Tioman, has been known to voyagers for over a thousand years when it served as a protected anchorage for ships plying the ancient spice route to China.
Right: Water villages along Sabah's coastline are inhabited by the Bajau Laut, the so-called Sea Gypsies who formerly lived an entirely nomadic life in their boats.

Top: Malaysia's tropical produce includes bananas, soursop and pineapples.
Bottom: Along Sabah's coastal route, watermelon sellers employ a novel way of advertising their wares.
Right: Manicured tea bushes swathe the hills and valleys of Cameron Highlands, which is renowned for producing high-quality tea.

Mangrove-forested wetlands, only recently recognized as an important ecosystem, rim most of the Peninsula's west coast, as well as much of the coastlines of Sabah and Sarawak, while the east coast from Kelantan to Johor is almost one long, palm-fringed beach. There are hundreds of islands: even the idyllic Langkawi group, nestled next to Thailand in the far northwest, number almost 100, while the east coast islands range from dramatic, mountainous Tioman to the quintessential tropical isles of Perhentian. Sabah's islands are even more spectacular, with Sipadan, Malaysia's only oceanic island, recently voted the world's best dive spot.

There is not only great geographical variety, but also, despite its equatorial location, seasonal differences. I love to fly in to Kota Bharu during the monsoon months – a time of renewal – when the flooded rice fields of the lush Kelantan basin reflect the clouds like a mirror mosaic. Coconut palms arch over the endless beaches where the surf pounds the sands, and sea mists drift like a veil across the land. Then I return months later, when the fields are bronze with ripened grain, and the rainbow-coloured fishing boats can again put to sea, and I am awed at the way the land changes with the seasons.

At other times, I take the road to Muar, along the coastal route from Melaka to Johor, where durian trees tower over gaily painted wooden houses high on stilts, where frilly curtains flutter from long, open windows, and potted bougainvilleas dazzle with their shocking pink blooms. Once again, I join the long line of travellers and writers who have delighted over the aesthetic way the Malays – a sensitive and artistic people – have tamed the land, the seamless way their villages, or kampongs,

blend with their surroundings, the way they beautify even the roadsides or the local police station with ornamental trees and flowering shrubs. As though beauty is a way of life. Or was.

Over the last decade, taming the land has turned ugly. An exploding population, and the greed of developers, have seen hills bulldozed and wetlands filled in to accommodate seas of concrete row-house suburbs. Ill-conceived highland highways, overclearing for vegetable farms and rampant logging have triggered landslides in delicate mountain environments. Sometimes when I return to a beloved scene – a peaceful kampong, a fishing village, a lonely forest trail – I am anxious to see if it is still there. But luckily there are many Malaysians who share my anxieties and are doing something about it.

Drifting from the mist-enshrouded forests, the gibbon's hoots sound like the disembodied voices of jungle spirits. The ethereal, swirling mists, the haunting cries of birds and beasts, the old English-style stone bungalows with their tales to tell, all add to the aura of mystery of Fraser's Hill, the cool colonial retreat perched on a series of seven hills in the mountains of Pahang. This is a favourite place where, to me, the tamed and the untamed are still apart but somehow harmonize. Only time will tell if this unique balancing act can continue in the future.

Left, top: A villager checks the progress of his crop along Sabah's coastal rice belt.
Left, bottom: Off Tanjung Kling, near Melaka, this fishing platform and its spiked traps, known as a *kelong*, is the traditional way of catching anchovies along the Strait of Melaka.
Right: Fabulous views of the 98 islands surrounding the main island of Langkawi; clear, calm waters dotted with white sailboats, sandy, white beaches, and some of the most luxurious hotels in the world are among Langkawi's offerings.

> "My feelings warmed to the attractive people around me. They wore bright-coloured sarongs (or skirts), bare legs, bare chests, singlets or bajus (pyjama jackets). They were human and carefree, gay and good looking, untroubled in this luscious, lethargic country...."
>
> — Patrick Balfour, *Grand Tour* (1935)

MALAYSIA'S MELTING POT

Decades of voracious silverfish have disfigured their faces, but in the old framed photographs I can still make out King George and Queen Mary and the modernizer of Turkey, Kemal Attaturk. Under these historical portraits, stacked against the walls, are battered metal travelling trunks, and on the floor are woven grass mats, the belongings and bedding respectively of the aging occupants of the Mutthuppehtai Indian Muslim Association, some of whom, like octogenarian Fackeer Mohamad, have made these austere lodgings their home since the 1930s when they first migrated from India's Tamil Nadu to Penang.

To step into this crumbling old shophouse on Georgetown's King Street, is to turn the clock back — a journey through time which romantics like me live for. Nothing has changed here for decades. But even as I write, the fate of this historic lodge, and hundreds of other Georgetown premises, is in jeopardy. With the millennium-end repeal of the Rent Control Act, market forces are now threatening not only their existence, but also that of their multicultural residents. Georgetown is such a unique "living" city that World Heritage status is imperative.

King Street is a microcosm of Malaysia itself. There are clan houses, temples, artisans' workshops, corner coffee shops, lawyers' offices and textile shops, to name just a few. Several doors down from the Muslim lodge, in the inner courtyard of the Tua Pek Kong Temple, I meet a woman from Kuala Lumpur who is visiting her mother, the resident Buddhist nun, a shaven-headed, white-robed Chinese woman whose beatific smile attests to her calm enjoyment of the monastic life. Across the road in a tiny workshop, under the auspicious gaze of calendar deities, I spy an Indian goldsmith sitting cross-legged at his bench, engrossed in his trade, as he has done for over half a century. While taking a break at a roadside stall, drinking hot, sweet tea, I watch the passing parade: women swathed in saris sway along the street to Hindi music warbling from a CD shop; a Malay elder wearing a white Haji cap from Mecca peddles past on his way to the mosque, and a Chinese secretary in a leopard skin miniskirt totters past on platform heels.

Acehnese, Ambonese, Arabs, Armenians, Bataks, Bengalis, Boyanese, Bugis, Burmese, Cantonese, Ceylonese, Chulias, Europeans, Gujeratis, Hainanese, Hakkas, Hokkiens, Kafirs, Malabaris, Malayalis, Malays, Mandailings, Minangs, Parsis, Pathans, Portuguese, Punjabis, Rawas, Siamese, Sindhis, Tamils, Telugus and Teochews – these and others created cosmopolitan Penang, and before it Melaka, and with them evolved Malaysia's reputation as hosting the most diverse population in Asia.

This diversity is perhaps best described by Henri Fauconnier, the French planter turned writer, in his award-winning novel of the 1920s, *Soul of Malaya*: "Learning that the Malays were Mahommedans I had set sail for a sort of Algeria, but had landed in a Chinese city. Since my arrival I had lived in India. And suddenly I find myself in Polynesia." Eight decades on, Fauconnier's Malaya is in many respects unrecognizable, but the trilogy is still surprisingly apt: the cities are still predominantly Chinese, the west coast plantations still Indian, and the countryside still Malay (Polynesians being of the same roots as Malays).

Malaysia's demographics have much to do with both geography and history – interlaced with trade, migrations, shifting settlements, religion and colonialism. However, they are not always as complex as in the melting-pot port cities of old, or in urban hubs like Kuala Lumpur where contemporary immigrations from the village to the city are an ongoing process, much like when the Industrial Revolution first hit Europe.

Previous page, left: At a Penang cultural show, a Malay girl shows how gifts were once carried.
Previous, page, right: Girls get ready for a traditional performance at the Sarawak Cultural Village.
Opposite: Dressed in traditional Malay dress and velvet fez, young Malay boys gather at Penang's Esplanade to celebrate the Islamic New Year.
Below: At an Indian dry-goods shop in Melaka, an array of aromatic spices are bought by housewives who choose to grind their own curry powders.

Above: In Terengganu, and in other Malay-dominated states such as Kedah and Kelantan, macaques are trained from an early age to climb coconut palms and throw the fruit down to their masters.

Right: When the monsoon closes east coast ports for four months of the year, boatmen like this Kelantanese fisherman take the opportunity to paint and repair their vessels.

If the great colonial-inspired Chinese and Indian immigrations to provide workers for the rubber and tin industries had not occurred in the late 19th century, Peninsular Malaysia's population would probably look much like that of the "Malay-crescent" states of Kedah, Kelantan and Terengganu, where people other than Malays – usually the descendants of early Chinese and Indian traders – number less than 10 per cent.

As the dominant race of the Peninsula, and numbering a sizeable percentage of both Sabah's and Sarawak's population, the Malays have not only given their name to that of their country, but are the most widely settled of the world's peoples. Around three to four millennium ago, sailing their flimsy outriggers, they settled throughout island Southeast Asia and continued across the entire Pacific and Indian oceans from Easter Island to Madagascar.

It is often said that people make a place, and just as Malaysian cities and towns – from Kuching to Johor Bahru – project the thriving, non-stop, dauntless empiricism of their major traders, the Chinese, the Malay-dominated regions are renowned for their tranquil, easy-going lifestyles in sync with the seasons. On the coastal plains of Kedah and Kelantan, rice growing is still the occupation of choice, while along the beaches and estuaries of the entire east coast, fishing remains at the core of the Malay way of life. In the towns and cities, by contrast, the Malays, greatly helped by the government's economic restructuring policy following ethnic disturbances in 1969, have moved into bastions formerly dominated by the Chinese, and now play an important role in sectors such as education, industry, science, technology, banking and commerce.

Above, clockwise from top left: Malay portraits: the white skullcap of this elderly Malay from Penang denotes one who has performed the Haj at Mecca; a Kelantanese fisherman favours a batik head wrap; a Malay boy participates in a street procession; a batik cloth is used as a sunshade by this rice harvester from Melaka; a Malay schoolgirl wears a pretty pink headscarf; and a young girl refreshes herself with a drink of sugarcane juice.
Opposite: A descendant of the Malay chieftain who built this famous house a century ago in Merlimau, Melaka, sits on the veranda, which features ornamental glazed Art Nouveau tiles and decorative woodcarvings.

The second largest group of Peninsular peoples, the Chinese, are largely descended from immigrants from southern China, who came in search of greener pastures. Many started as labourers, small shopkeepers and merchants in the main towns and tin-mining centres – eventually prompting the formation of the ubiquitous Chinatowns – and they continue to dominate the business world. The third largest group, the Indians, were brought into Malaya mostly from southern Indian as contract labourers but, like the Chinese, many ventured into trade while others worked in government. These peoples – and others – have contributed to the wonderfully complex tapestry of Malaysia their language, customs, dress, religions, cuisine and architectural heritage.

From the Kadazandusun of Sabah's Mount Kinabalu to the nomadic Penan of the rainforests, from the sea-roving Bajau Laut to the longhouse-dwelling Iban, from the sago-growing Melanau to the rice-growing Kelabit, these and all the other diverse peoples of Malaysian Borneo are from the same racial roots as the Malays, known by the majority of anthropologists and prehistorians as Austronesians. But where they first came from is a matter of heated debate in academic circles: the two main theories are that they descend from Pleistocene populations who could have walked across the land bridges then joining Borneo and Southeast Asia between 18,000 and 10,000 years ago, or that they were the original inhabitants of Taiwan who arrived in Malaysia, perhaps by sea, around 4,000 years ago.

They were not the first inhabitants, however. Excavations in both Peninsular Malaysia and Sarawak have revealed skeletal remains that appear to be closely related to Aboriginal Australians and Melanesians – the Austro-Melanesians. They

mysteriously disappeared in Borneo, but behind the Peninsula's coastal realms, in the interior of the mountainous forests, still live remnant bands of hunters and gatherers known as Negritos, who in all probability descended from these earliest inhabitants.

Language is the litmus test of origin. The Negritos and most of the Orang Asli agriculturalists of the Peninsula, such as the 40,000-strong Senoi, speak Austroasiatic languages unrelated to Austronesian languages like Malay, but similar to that of ancient Cambodia. Perhaps, over the millennia, they gradually made their way over mainland Southeast Asia to arrive in the Malay Peninsula – in the way that peoples have been doing ever since.

Across the South China Sea, in Borneo, there is a different kind of anthropological debate – whether the nomads preceded the agriculturalists or vice versa. Some scholars think that the present nomadic Penan abandoned their settled life for the forest, while others believe that Borneo's inland peoples, like the Kenyah, were once rainforest dwellers who became agriculturalists. Sabah, it appears, never had nomads, at least of the forest variety, but the last of the Bajau Laut, or Sea Gypsies, have only in recent times given up their sea nomad existence, although they still build their houses perched on stilts over the sea.

They are not the only ones to give up their old ways. For everywhere in Malaysia, traditional lifestyles are being exchanged for contemporary ones, and nowhere, not even the

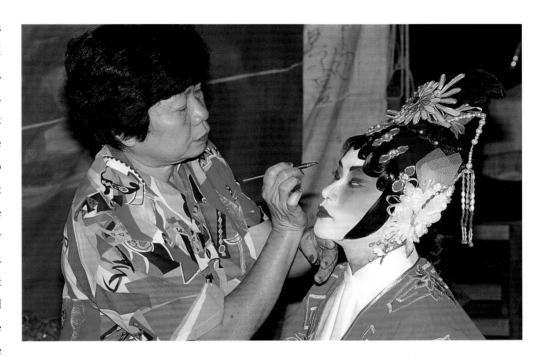

Left: As the sun goes down, Petaling Street, Malaysia's most famous street market in Kuala Lumpur's Chinatown, comes alive with a sea of hawkers.
Right, top: Its traditions relatively unchanged for over a millennium, Chinese opera is still performed on important festive occasions.
Right, bottom: This calligrapher in a Chinese temple in Melaka is busiest at Chinese New Year when homes are decorated with lucky messages.

Above, left to right: Indians, who make up 10 per cent of Malaysia's population, zealously uphold their cultural traditions. An upper-caste Brahmin at an Indian temple in Kuala Lumpur; an Indian child participates in the annual Thaipusam celebrations; and wearing her best sari, a young woman comes to worship at a temple.
Right: Indian shops, such as this one in Kuala Lumpur's Leboh Ampang, are colourful affairs, stocking everything from religious calendars to bananas.

most remote village or longhouse, escapes the pervasive call of the urban bright lights. A traditional Kadazan dancer in Sabah admits that she is about to join her sister in a Johor factory producing microchips; and similar tales abound throughout the rural areas. It is all about economics. The only ones who can stay are those with enough land to survive or those who can somehow find a way to combine their age-old way of life with the curse and saviour of traditional communities — tourism.

Despite this, most Malaysians manage to keep up some of their traditions in a unique mélange that combines the old with the new: a Kelantanese masseur wears a traditional head wrap but takes bookings on his mobile phone; a Rungus tribesman creates a bamboo longhouse but ferries tourists there in a minivan; a Malay politician relies on Western medicine for a heart bypass but will visit the shaman to plot his rival's downfall; a Chinese businessman drives the latest Mercedes but stops on the superhighway to buy coconut milk-soaked glutinous rice cooked in bamboo in the aboriginal style; while at the Sarawak Cultural Village, the "actors" lead dual lives, dressing and taking part in their forefathers' lifestyle by day and coming home to modern life after work. Even at the old Muslim guild in Georgetown, Nordin, the youngest lodger, has installed a television at the head of his sleeping mat, to share space with the fading portraits and the old tin trunks.

Left: Found in the southwest corner of Sarawak, the Bidayuh are renowned for their creative use of bamboo, especially in their traditional longhouses. The veranda is reserved for communal activities such as pounding rice and weaving mats. This longhouse has been reconstructed at the Sarawak Cultural Village outside of Kuching.

Above, clockwise from top left: All of Sarawak's indigenous people are Austronesians, but comprise more than a dozen major ethnic groups, whose cultural traditions and clothing are as colourful as they are various: an Iban youth dons a beaded cap for festivals; a Malay girl wears a headscarf embroidered with gold thread; the Penan have basin-style haircuts; an Iban girl wears a beaded vest in a hornbill design; another Iban dons an elaborate feathered headdress; and a Kayan woman is among the last to practise the fashion of stretched earlobes.

Above, left to right: Sabah's multicultural peoples don their original clothing only on festive occasions. The Rungus are the last of Sabah's longhouse dwellers; the Bajau are often called the "Cowboys of the East"; and the Kadazan create haunting tunes on bamboo pipes.

Left: In Kampung Penambawan, Bajau children return from school along the wooden walkways that connect the houses of their water village.

THE SPIRIT OF ART

In sun-drenched rooms, chrome yellow mangoes tempt the palate on a purple table, lime green leaves sprout from an ultramarine vase, and pink sandals are cast aside on a red floor. Like images from a tropical dream, evoking warmer, more sensual climes, these are the kind of interiors you dream of when deep in winter blues.

"Roomscapes", their creator, Rafiee Ghani, one of Malaysia's hottest artists, calls them. Not surprisingly, he derives much of his inspiration for his oil paintings from a childhood spent in Kelantan, the northeastern state known as the heartland of Malay culture. Here, along the lanes that wind through rice fields and past palm-fringed beaches, are hundreds of family-run workshops where stamped and hand-painted batik, handwoven silks, woodcarvings, silverware, shadow puppets and kites are produced. Here, even the fishing boats are adorned with carved figureheads and painted in rainbow colours.

Half a century ago, the travel writer Norman Lewis commented, when visiting a Burmese village, that "art is sometimes protected by poverty, and civilization can be the destroyer of taste". It is a sweeping generalization, but in some ways a correct one, no matter where. It is also true for Malaysia.

It is no coincidence that the least developed regions are the richest in traditional arts and crafts. Cut off from the west coast by rugged mountains, and isolated during the monsoon, the east coast states of Kelantan and Terengganu were scarcely touched by colonialism, leaving many of their customs and arts intact.

In Borneo, there was a different scenario. Although Sarawak was ruled by the Brookes, by keeping local laws and discouraging Western intervention, many crafts, including handwoven ikat textiles, woodcarvings, basketry and beadwork, still survived. In Sabah, the colonial administrators were more interested in profits than in traditions, so that crafts like beadwork, weaving and basketry survived only through necessity and isolation.

From prehistoric cave murals to contemporary oil paintings, Malaysia's arts and crafts are the evolution of local traditions and outside influences. In Terengganu, I notice house designs that reflect Thai influences. In Kelantan, I see Javanese trends in their shadow puppets. In Melaka, tile work borrows from both Chinese

Previous page, left: The *kenyalang*, a painted woodcarving symbolizing the hornbill, is sacred to the Iban, who believe it is a messenger from the spirit world.
Previous page, right: Sarawak's Orang Ulu are gifted craftsmen. Painted swirling patterns are used to decorate bark cloth jackets and woodwork.
Left: Newly dyed batik sarongs hang from clotheslines strung between coconut palms in the villages around Kota Bharu, Kelantan.
Right: Hand-painted batik is a speciality of cottage craft industries centred around Pantai Cahaya Bulan, north of Kota Bharu.

Above: Iban ritual textiles, known as *pua kumbu*, are handwoven using the warp ikat, or tie–dye, method. Designs are inspired by Iban animistic beliefs, the spiritual realm and the natural world. *Pua kumbu* weaving is the preserve of Iban women, who have high status in their community and who pass their skills down to their daughters.

Right: The "cloth of gold", as *songket* is often called, is the most costly of all Malaysian textiles. Terengganu is famous for its fine *songket*, including these antique and contemporary weavings that are among the collection of Tengku Ismail bin Tengku Su, the Terengganu prince who has done much to rejuvenate the art of fine *songket* weaving.

and European styles, while batik, now the most characteristic and well known of Malaysian crafts, was introduced from Indonesia only in the 1930s.

In a museum in Taiping, Perak, I find stone tools dating from 40 millennia ago, and evidence of Malaysia's first artistic renaissance, during the Neolithic era around 2000 BC, when pottery and polished stone tools appeared. In the Sarawak Museum, there are tricolor burial urns from the Niah Caves that were produced using the same methods employed by Iban potters today. But mystery still surrounds many artefacts and their creators and the reasons behind some of the creations – such as the megaliths that appear in both Borneo and along the Peninsula's west coast.

Stone endures the longest, but woodwork has been around for probably just as long. Home to the oldest rainforests in the world, it is no wonder that Malaysia has a rich and ongoing tradition of woodcarving. It is a craft that is steeped in custom. Some carvers still say special prayers to gain permission from the resident spirits before entering the forest and felling the trees, an obvious precaution given the size of some of these giants.

The last time I visited Pion anak Bumbon, master woodcarver of the Mah Meri people, at his Carey Island home off the coast of Selangor, he was out searching for a special tree that is becoming increasingly hard to find with the clearing of mangrove forests for oil palm plantations. While I watched his contemporaries chiselling away at their "spirit" carvings – once used

Left: Renowned Malaysian chef, Shukri Shafie, constructed his traditional Kedah-style house on Langkawi Island in line with ancient rites and ceremonies. The carvings on the fascia boards and in the panels above and below the louvred shutters take their design inspiration from local spices.

for drawing bad spirits out of people but now popular with collectors of primitive art – Pion unexpectedly returned; he knew he had visitors because he felt a tic in his eyelid. Following tradition, Pion's mastery comes both from his talent and the uncanny way he is in sync with the spiritual world, a dualism that in the old days was expected of craftsmen possessing great ability.

Likewise with the famed shadow puppeteer Hamzah. Once when I was visiting him at his home outside Kota Bharu, a family came to ask him to help cure their young daughter who was refusing to eat. He unhesitatingly agreed, and I was witness to a timeless ceremony where Hamzah took over as his alter ego – the village *bomoh*, or traditional healer.

Spirits are also called upon in house building when the main post, once believed to be the receptacle of the "soul" of the house, is raised. This ceremony is seldom seen these days, but on Langkawi Island I meet with Shukri bin Shafie, who constructed his beautiful wooden home in accordance with all the ancient ceremonies. His concern for the dwindling numbers of traditional houses, and the loss of Malay customs and heritage, has translated into a conscious and tangible move to save them.

Shukri inherited his love of tradition from his grandmother, whose expertise in everything from herbal medicines to ceremonial rituals was often utilized by the royal family of Kedah. She, of course, followed a long line of skilled workers and artisans who once found employment in Malaysia's royal courts.

Right: At the woodcarving atelier of A. Rahman in Binjai, near Kota Bharu, a craftsman creates a carved panel decorated with an arabesque of intertwining leaves and flowers. The carving in the foreground features a Qur'anic inscription set amidst foliage.

Royal patronage, and the constant cycle of weddings and other celebrations, meant that silk weavers, silver- and gold-smiths, woodcarvers and metal workers lived in and around the royal courts. Kelantan's court was famed for its gold and silver craftsmen, while Terengganu was renowned for its *songket*, a handwoven silk shot with designs in silver and gold thread that was once the prerogative of royalty. Today, it is the favoured dress for Malay weddings and official functions, although certain colours are still indicative of royal status. These are explained to me by Tengku Ismail, often known as the "prince of songket", who not only engineered the revitalization of Terengganu's famed cloth but also follows the age-old royal tradition, the involvement of nobles in the production of crafts, a practice that was first recorded in the courtly annals of the 15th-century Melakan sultanate.

In Sabah and Sarawak, there was no tradition of royal patronage. Arts and crafts were created by each member of the household as essential everyday items. People as diverse as the Rungus from northwestern Sabah, and the Iban from Sarawak's great rivers, all used the backstrap loom to produce outstanding woven textiles. The nomadic Penan and the riverine Kayan wove an assortment of intricate baskets from rainforest fibres, while the Orang Ulu and Melanau carved totem-like pillars to hold the coffins of their ancestors.

While crafts were a part of everyday life, patterns were de-rived from the spirit world, producing imagery that makes these

Left: Nik Mohd Noh bin Abdullah, one of Kelantan's most famous kite makers, creates his wind machines from fine bamboo frames covered with coloured paper at his house at Kampung Penampang.

crafts so popular with serious collectors. At the same time, it has also, according to a Sabahan who is passionate about reviving Kadazandusun traditions, contributed to their destruction. Even today, Christian fundamentalist missionaries insist that successful conversion can only be accomplished by destroying all symbolic belongings, including textiles and carvings.

But it is not only religious fervour that destroys age-old arts. Nowadays, it is difficult to find any Borneans wearing traditional dress for everyday use, while plastic has replaced organic fibres. Change has been apparent for at least a century since factory-made goods filtered through during the colonial days.

At the same time, however, the introduction of oil painting and watercolours has seen the rise of many fine painters such as Ibrahim Hussein, Latiff Mohidin and Syed Amad Jamal, who combine their Malay-Islamic traditions with Western techniques to create striking abstracts.

Others, too, know how to use change to their advantage. Many of Malaysia's most stunning resorts have utilized traditional Malay house design to great acclaim. Rungus weavers still use backstrap looms but now create goods for tourists. Mah Meri carvers still use designs based on their pantheon of spirits to make sculptures to adorn apartments. Meanwhile, there is a new breed of painters, like Harris Ribut who creates his "fat lady" series of rotund women wrapped in batik sarongs from scenes of his childhood, and Rafiee Ghani who charms those who see in his colour-charged roomscapes a place of their dreams.

Right: A Kelantanese *tok dalang*, the puppeteer and narrator of the shadow puppet theatre, or *wayang kulit*, holds aloft two famous characters from the great Indian epic, the *Ramayana*.

Left: At the Sarawak Cultural Village, an Iban weaver creates a traditional fabric on a simple backstrap loom, while a craftswoman in the background makes conical bamboo sunhats covered with beads. Split bamboo mats cover the floor.
Above, clockwise from top left: Bornean crafts are colourful, intricate and symbolic: a woven Iban vest, or *kelambi*, patterned with omen birds; a piece of Orang Ulu beadwork featuring a spirit design known as "the tree of life"; an array of modern bead necklaces in traditional designs; and double-sided, traditional embroidered headdresses of the Rungus people of Sabah.

Above, clockwise from top left: Until recently, with the advent of plastic, basketry was a craft of necessity, and Sarawak's basket weavers produced an enormous range of products, from multipurpose mats to a wide variety of baskets. Multicoloured baskets are now produced for the tourist market, but in many upriver areas baskets are still used in daily activities: for holding seeds, for winnowing and fishing, for storage, and for carrying heavy loads along mountainous paths.

Right: Rafiee Ghani, one of Malaysia's top contemporary artists, evokes tropical dreams in his richly coloured oil paintings.

"And when Makhdum Saiyid Abdul-Aziz had finished his prayers, the Raja made his elephant kneel and he mounted the Makhdum on the elephant and took him to the palace. And the Bendahara and the chiefs embraced Islam, and every citizen of Malaka, whether of high or low degree, was commanded by the Raja to do likewise."

— C. C. Brown (translator), *Sejarah Melayu or Malay Annals* (1952)

GREAT FAITHS IN UNISON

The evening began like any other in my Kuala Lumpur apartment, but it was a moment in time that I shall always remember as my epiphany of multi-devotional Malaysia. As usual, at sundown, I heard the sonorous call of the muezzin floating from the minaret of the nearby mosque, and almost in unison the ringing of bells for evening *puja* in the Hindu temple only a block away. Then, the evening suddenly became magically different. I heard delighted screams coming from the playground, and looking down I noticed children running about trailing glowing paper lanterns made in the shape of fish and dragons, for that evening they were celebrating the Mooncake Festival in honour of an ancient Chinese peasant victory over Mongolian warlords.

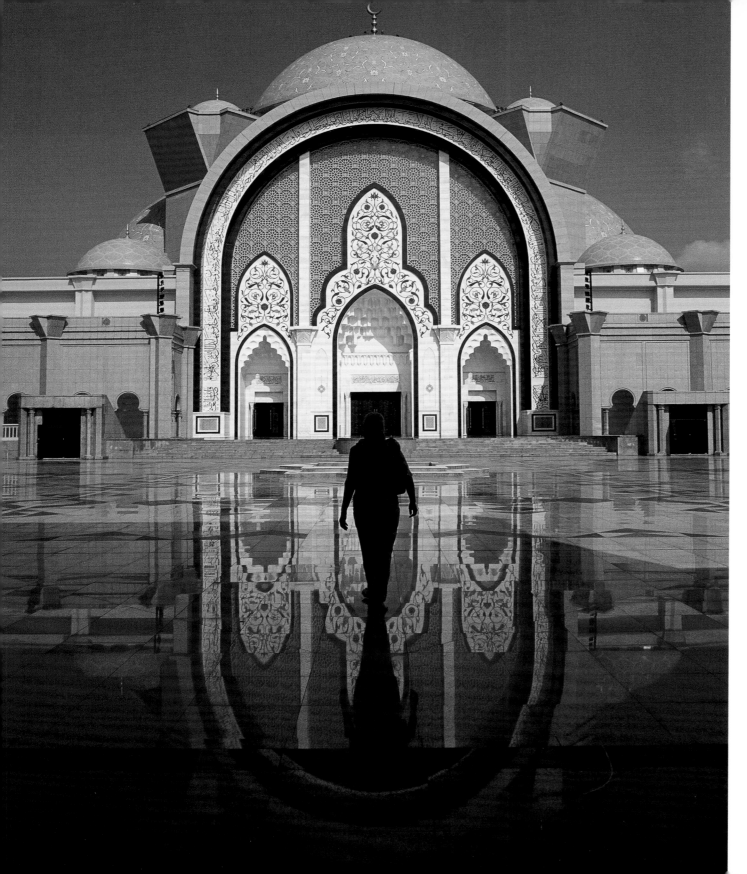

Previous page, left: Guardians from Chinese legends are immortalized on the doors of a Penang temple.

Previous page, right: Selangor's State Mosque at Shah Alam, the Sultan Salahuddin Abdul Aziz Shah Mosque, features the world's tallest minarets and a computer-designed dome.

Left: An enormous marble-paved fore-court and intricate inlays of arabesques in coloured marble are among the archi-tectural delights of Kuala Lumpur's Wilayah Mosque.

Opposite, top: Built in 1965, the National Mosque features colourful stained-glass windows in the Great Hall, and a faceted roof which echoes the design of the main roof of the mosque.

Opposite, bottom: Keeping the dome shining is a demanding job for workers at Sabah's Ranau Mosque.

As far as Malaysians are concerned, the spectacle of the rituals of various faiths enacted at the same time in the same place is commonplace, but for outsiders it is not only unusual, but in these days of mounting religious tensions in the rest of the world, it is indeed unforgettable.

At a glance, it is evident that Western-style progress has been enthusiastically embraced in the country, but religion is still the guiding force for most of the population. A walk down any street in Malaysia, or a drive through the countryside will indeed show that religion is very much a part of everyday life. It will also show that the devotional make-up of Malaysia is as diverse as its population. It is also a tribute to the racial tolerance of Malaysia's peoples that such diverse religions can exisit side by side. With all the world's major faiths represented, as well as a wide array of minor ones, Malaysians are the lucky recipients of more public holidays than practically any other people in the world.

Although freedom of worship of all faiths is preserved in the constitution, the one that lingers in the mind as being essentially Malaysian is Islam, the national faith. Once, when I was talking with my sister on a long-distance telephone call from Australia, she heard the *azan*, the call to prayer, in the background, and was instantly overcome with a longing to visit; for her, this sound was the essence of Malaysia.

Five times a day, from the minarets of some of the world's most spectacular mosques down to the humble wooden prayer houses of the kampong, the call to prayer is answered by around two-thirds of the nation's population – the majority Malays, as well as Indian Muslims, th^e majority of coastal peoples in

Borneo, including the Bajau and Orang Sungai of Sabah and the Melanau of Sarawak, and other small pockets of converts, from Chinese to Kadazan.

Islam is portrayed with such bias in much of the Western media that it comes as a surprise to most non-Muslims when they learn that it means "The Way of Peace". To best see Islam in this light, there is no better place to start than Malaysia, where the way of Mohammad was introduced not by the sword but by trade. Initiated, probably in the 15th century by wealthy Arab and Indian merchants, Islam's revolutionary concept that all men are equal, where the sultan can kneel beside the poorest of his subjects to pray, must have had powerful psychological advantages in this feudal land.

When V. S. Naipaul, the acerbic novelist, wrote *Among the Believers*, he caused quite a controversy by declaring that the further one went from the source of Islam – Arabia – the less intense the religion became. It was a sweeping and highly uninformed statement considering his breezy acquaintance with most countries he visited. Nevertheless, there is no denying that Malaysian Islam is certainly different to that of the Middle East. This, however, has more to do with culture, climate and geography than with any lack of fervour.

Malay women dress in traditional, long, loose attire, but nothing like the sombre garb of their Middle Eastern sisters, for

Left: To celebrate Awal Muharram, the Islamic New Year, Penang's Muslim public servants don matching outfits and hold aloft tinselled "trees", or *bunga manggar*, for a procession through the streets.
Right: A trio of Malay schoolboys visit Kuala Lumpur's Islamic Arts Museum with its splendid domes topped by tiled arabesques and encircled by Qur'anic verses, created by Uzbekhistan craftsmen.

Left: At Penang's Burmese Temple in Burma Lane, an aura of serentity prevails as worshippers place lighted candles in front of a Buddha image seated on a lotus "bud" framed by a filagree metal archway.

Above: For the Mooncake Festival, which celebrates the overthrow of the Mongol warlords in ancient China, mooncakes are exchanged and children carry colourful paper lanterns.

here colourful batik and sensuous silks combine with flowing scarves to create the most striking of Southeast Asian everyday dress. While men usually wear Western dress, on Fridays, the Muslim day of prayer, and at festive times and for celebrations, they change into their elegant, silky pantsuits with matching brocade sarongs and velvet fez.

Malaysian mosques are strikingly evident throughout the country and offer a wonderful diversity of styles and regional variations. Outside of Kota Bharu, I am struck by the simplicity of the nation's oldest wooden mosque at Kampung Laut. In Melaka, I am puzzled by the oddity of the pagoda-style minarets on the 18th-century Terengkera and Kampong Kling mosques. South of Kuala Terengganu, I am awed by the beauty of the "floating mosque" reflected in the lagoon at sunset. In the nation's capital, I am mesmerized by the grandiosity of Kuala Lumpur's Wilayah Mosque spotlit at dusk, and in the sleepy royal town of Kuala Kangsar, I am dazzled by the golden onion domes that dominate the Ubudiah Mosque, where work was interrupted when a rogue elephant smashed the marble tiles.

An old Malay proverb, *Biar mati anak, jangan mati adat*, meaning "lose a child rather than a custom", is evidence of the importance of Malay customs, many of which are a unique combination of cultural layers, such as the wedding ceremony

Left: On Vesak Day, commemorating Buddha's birth, enlightenment and his achievement of Nirvana, even children participate by making offerings at Buddhist temples.
Opposite: At Kuala Lumpur's Batu Caves, and in Penang, Thaipusam, the Hindu festival in honour of Lord Subramaniam, attracts thousands of tranced penitents who climb to the clifftop shrine carrying *kavadi*, ritual offerings attached to their bodies with hooks.

where rituals derive from pre-Islamic Hindu customs. Even older traces can be found in the chants of traditional healers and in the still popular belief in ghosts and spirits.

In the beginning, spirits dwelt everywhere – in the seas, rivers, lakes and mountains, and even in rocks and trees – and these had to be constantly appeased for they were in control of all the natural forces. In traditional agricultural societies, it was a disaster if the rains failed. Even today, during droughts, special prayers are held at mosques, and traditional shamans are called upon to invoke the rains, or in some cases, keep them away – such as at important outdoor events, including the opening ceremony for the 1998 Commonwealth Games.

A successful harvest was, and still is, cause for celebration. In Sarawak and Sabah, where the annual harvest festivals have become public holidays, they are occasions for great merry-making even though most of the Iban, Kadazandusun, Kenyah and Kayan have long embraced Christianity. There are, though, still small groups of Orang Asli on the Peninsula, and upriver tribes in Malaysian Borneo who still follow the ways of their ancestors and practise a variety of indigenous religions. Here, spirits are a major concern, and much care is taken to attract the favour of well-disposed spirits and to placate or expel spirits which threaten harm through age-old rituals conducted by religious specialists such as bards, priests, shamans and priestess-mediums. Here, too, bird augury is still widely observed.

But the most prominent adherents of ancestor worship are the Chinese, who number almost a third of Malaysia's population. Their devotions are also the most visible, for not only are temples found in every Malaysian town, but there are also clan

Left: Indian women pose beneath the *gopuram*, the towering archway decorated with statues of deities that identifies temples built in the Tamil style of southern India.
Below: A detail from the *gopuram* at Kuala Lumpur's Sri Mahamariamman Temple.
Opposite: Relatives and friends crowd the Hindu temple at Ampang, Selangor, for a traditional wedding.

houses with shrines, household altars in living rooms open to the street, and even small tin altars attached to the veranda columns outside shophouses. At all of these, every day of the year, joss sticks are burnt and offerings made.

Malaysian Chinese can be Taoists, Buddhists, Confucianists, or sometimes a mixture of all, and their festivals are noisy, colourful affairs, when spirits must be propitiated in order to bring good luck, and elaborate offerings ensure that their ancestors' ghosts are appeased. Superstition and symbolism pervade all aspects of life. During the Lunar New Year, the colour red, signifying prosperity, is lavishly used in clothing and in the banners inscribed with good luck slogans which are draped across buildings. Extra long noodles are also eaten to ensure long life, and noisy lion dances are staged to expel evil spirits.

In Kuala Lumpur, I enter the smoke-enshrouded Sze Ya Temple, where an altar honours Yap Ah Loy, the city's pioneering headman. In Penang, famed for its temples, I stop by to feed the flocks of pigeons in the courtyard of the popular Goddess of Mercy Temple, I climb the steps to the top of the 10,000 Buddhas Precious Pagoda for a stunning view of the Kek Lok Si, Malaysia's largest Buddhist temple, and I visit the Khoo Kongsi, perhaps the most ornate Chinese clanhouse in the world, where porcelain dragons cavort across the roof and every surface is either gilded, carved, enamelled, tiled or painted.

Hinduism was the first of the world's great religions to arrive in Southeast Asia, and ancient artefacts unearthed from Kedah, Perak and Sarawak, together with Hindu customs that survive in Malaysia's royal courts, are evidence that it had a pervasive and long-lasting influence. But apart from small groups of traders in

Melaka and Penang, Malaysia's Indian community, numbering some 10 per cent of the population, dates from the great immigrations during the late 19th and early 20th centuries when labourers from southern India came to work on rubber plantations. Enter any Indian temple and you are transported to the subcontinent: magnificent towering archways, or *gopuram*, encrusted with deities, echo those of Tamil Nadu, while the customs, celebrations, dress and lifestyle of their motherland are still faithfully followed by local Indians. During Thaipusam, a major Hindu festival held in honour of Lord Subramaniam, penitents pray and fast before taking part in processions to hill temples, some, in trance, carrying massive *kavadi*, ornate frames supported by metal spikes inserted in their bodies.

In Melaka, I have followed the Catholic descendants of the Portuguese conquistadors in the candlelit Easter procession. In Kelantan, I have looked on while a shaman evoked the spirits to cure a sick child. I have watched sacred snakes writhing around altars in a Penang temple, and seen tranced Buddhists walking across hot coals during the Festival of the Nine Emperor Gods. For the last fifteen years, I have joined in the greatest of the world's mass events, the month-long Muslim fast of Ramadan, and rejoiced at its end when Muslims nationwide throw open their houses for a month of celebration. Only in Malaysia.

Left: A visit to a longhouse is an unforgettable experience, providing a glimpse into the communal lifestyle of the Iban or Orang Ulu. Longhouse entertainments often include traditional war dances, such as the Iban's hornbill dance, accompanied by the beat of drums and gongs.
Right: At Sabah's Monosopiad Cultural Village, built and maintained by the descendants of the famous Kadazan warrior of the same name, musicians entertain with a traditional gong performance.

"Now you think you have exhausted Malaya. Nonsense. No country can be disappointing if you explore the depths of it. Satiety is a disease of the tourist. You must know how to turn over the page. The world, even the smallest corner of it, is a Book of the Thousand and One Nights."

— Henri Fauconnier, *The Soul of Malaya* (1931)

THE COLOURS
OF MALAYSIA

For those who believe in mystic coincidence, it would probably not seem in the least unusual that the first time I visited Asia, back in the days when sea travel was cheaper than air, I arrived from Australia on a cruise ship called the SS *Malaysia*. Little did I know then that I was later to spend half of my adult life in that very country.

I was on my way overland on the "hippie trail" through Asia to Europe, and my foray through Malaysia was as memorable as it was brief. It was tinted with the rose-coloured glasses of the innocence of youth, but the cameos remain as vivid today as then: the domes of Kuala Lumpur's old railway station silhouetted at sunset, the chaotic excitement of a Chinatown night market, the climb up the cliff face to a Hindu temple at Batu Caves, cycling around Penang's northern beaches, hitching a ride in a Mercedes, and burrowing through rubber plantations and oil palm estates on the mail train.

When I returned in 1985, to carry out research for a book, I took up rooms for a few months in an old Chinese mansion overlooking the sea at Melaka. From there I could look out across the placid straits, smell the briny tropical air, and sometimes on the horizon spot an Indonesian prau sailing past on the trade winds like a phantom from the past.

I had a bag of books with me, all on Malaysia, and most of these were authored by outsiders, visitors like myself. Their impressions and accounts of this exotic land made for wonderful reading, and have continued to inspire me as well as anyone who visits, whether in person or in the imagination.

Some travellers come for history and find it in the crooked lanes of Melaka and Georgetown. Others come for adventure and find it on the slopes of Mount Kinabalu and deep in the rainforests. Yet others are lured by the spicy cuisine of Penang and the wondrous array of tropical fruits. Some head for the luxurious resorts of Langkawi and Pangkor or the colonial inns of Cameron Highlands and Fraser's Hill. Some need the tranquility of the countryside, while others crave the heat, noise and excitement of Kuala Lumpur. Most just want to escape the monotony of everyday life and journey to somewhere that, however familiar it may seem on the surface, is really very different.

Previous page, left: Menara Kuala Lumpur, a 421-foot-high communications tower, provides a bird's-eye view of Malaysia's capital.
Previous page, right: With its Moorish-style architecture and gleaming copper domes, the majestic Sultan Abdul Samad Building in Kuala Lumpur is just as impressive as when it was built over a century ago.
Left and right: Kuala Lumpur City Centre, the capital's vital new heart, boasts not only the Petronas Twin Towers, but also the spectacular Suria shopping mall and a beautifully landscaped park and pools where children cool off in the tropical heat.

Like me, one of my favourite writers, the Victorian adventuress Isabella Bird, was always looking for a chance to escape. But when she journeyed through the Malay Peninsula, back in 1879, it was very different. Travellers, especially Englishwomen, were extremely scarce then. She was also a rare and indomitable individual whose perceptive and engaging descriptions are as real today as they were then. When she writes of sailing past the Dindings, now known as Pangkor, she describes the main island as "unspeakably lovely as it lay in the golden light between us and the sun, forest-covered to its steep summit, its rocky promontories running out into calm, deep, green water … margined by shores of white coral sand backed by dense groves of coco-palms whose curving shadows lay dark upon the glassy sea". Over a century later, when the famous singer Luciano Pavarotti visited its tiny sister isle of Pangkor Laut, with its renowned luxury resort, he was equally moved, commenting, "I almost cried when I saw how beautiful God made this paradise."

Bird, again similar to me, was sociable to a degree, but after an urban stint, could hardly wait, as she put it, to once again "head for the wilds". Then, the great rainforests blanketed the land from coast to coast. Rivers were the only thoroughfares, there were few roads, and on inland forays she rode on elephant back. She was encumbered by Victorian dress, "malignantly bitten" by mosquitoes, but even sitting in a shack by the "teeming

Left, top: Portuguese dancers, the descendants of Melaka's 16th-century conquerors, perform an Iberian dance at Merdeka Square.
Left, bottom: Bintang Walk, a pedestrian mall in the heart of Kuala Lumpur's shopping district, is a favourite place to gather after dark.
Right: Sunway Lagoon Resort, with its wave pool and nearby shopping mall, is a popular place to stay while visiting Kuala Lumpur.

slime and swamp" of Klang she managed to not only keep her spirits high, but also to record her every impression, some of which are as true today as when she penned them. Klang, she wrote, "does not improve on further aquaintance", while Kuala Kangsar was her favourite place in all of Asia. She was Eurocentric, and utterly Victorian, but unusual for her time she was one of the first to warn against the dangers of British intervention. She found great beauty in everything, from traditional Malay houses to statuesque Indian women dressed in their saris, which to her were much more suitable than fashionable European garb that distorted women's figures into "the shape of a Japanese sake bottle … impeding motion, and affecting health, comfort, and beauty alike".

A frequent visitor was Somerset Maugham, who more than any author created the Malayan myth of colonial indolence – of long, tropical evenings and intrigues – that is still a potent lure, contributing to the success of everything from "grand hotels" like Kuala Lumpur's Carcosa Seri Negara and Penang's E & O, to nostalgic train journeys like the luxury Eastern & Oriental and the quaint steam train of the North Borneo Railway.

Maugham's Tanah Merah is Melaka thinly disguised, and

Left: The Khoo Kongsi is not only Penang's but Malaysia's most famous and elaborate clanhouse. Designed in the style of an imperial palace, every available surface is sumptuously carved, gilded, painted, tiled or enamelled. The roof is adorned with porcelain dragons and flowers.
Right, top: Penang's Kek Lok Si Temple, Malaysia's largest temple complex, is located in an auspicious position on a hillside at Ayer Itam. The complex was built in 1904, although the main pagoda dates from 1930.
Right, bottom: Recent winner of a Unesco award for conservation, the Cheong Fatt Tze Mansion, a 38-room Chinese courtyard mansion on Penang's Lebuh Leith, has been faithfully restored to its former glory, complete with blue paintwork, and now hosts a boutique hotel.

Above: Visitors to Melaka can opt for a change of pace with a ride on a traditional bullock cart, known locally as a *kereta lembu*.
Opposite: Melaka's Town Square contains some of Malaysia's most historic buildings, including the Dutch-built, 18th-century Christ Church (centre) and the massive 17th-century Stadthuys, the former residence of the Dutch governor and the town's civil administration building (right). To the left of the church is the town's former post office, built in Dutch style in 1931, which now houses the Youth Museum. The fountain was built in 1904 to commemorate the Diamond Jubilee of Queen Victoria's reign.

when you wander the streets of the old quarter, dismissing the ugliness of the new town, you can still feel that "It has the sad and romantic air of all places that have once been of importance and live now on the recollection of a vanished grandeur."

But more than the grandeur of the country was disappearing by the time Anthony Burgess, who worked as a teacher in colonial Malaya and Borneo from 1954 to 1960, wove his experiences into his book, *The Long Day Wanes: A Malayan Trilogy*. Even then, "the romantic dream he had entertained" was over. "The whole East was awake, building dams and canals, power-houses and car factories."

Travellers today will see some of what Maugham and Bird saw, as well as much of what Burgess predicted. If you arrive at the new Kuala Lumpur International Airport, get whisked in a limo along superhighways past seas of satellite suburbs capped with the world's tallest buildings, you will wonder whatever happened to Maugham's Malaya. For some people, it does not matter. They can spend their time marvelling at some of Asia's most astounding contemporary architecture, shop till they drop in huge malls that rival the West's, and wonder at the success of globalization where hotel chains provide identical service and even Big Macs taste the same.

But despite tourism bodies and advertisements touting the nation's safety, development and progress, the plasticized charms of Starbucks and The Coffee Bean pall before that of a traditional corner coffee shop, the food court at the mall has nothing on a *laksa* or *teh tarik* stall by the beach, and even the best department store cannot compete with the pleasures of an open-air market under the stars.

Much, however, is fast disappearing. Ancestral houses in the kampong have been abandoned by families who migrate to the city for work. Once quiet rural roads are now jammed with traffic, the result of a more than successful national car industry. Factory-produced goods have crowded out local crafts at markets, and television and DVDs have long ago replaced shadow-puppet theatres.

For the majority who travel as I do, for the romance, the thrill of finding yourself alone in a totally different environment, where everything, even the light and colour are unfamiliar, there are still many places in Malaysia that offer unequalled delights. But these days you just have to search a little harder to find them.

Left: A typically narrow-fronted, elongated Melakan townhouse in Jonkers Street, now converted to a restaurant, provides a perfect setting for Nonya cuisine, the speciality of Straits-born Chinese women. The decorative elements inside the townhouse, much influenced by the Dutch and British colonial presence in Melaka, echo the spicy and piquant blend of Malay ingredients and Chinese cooking styles which are characteristic of the popular Nonya cuisine.

Above, clockwise from top left: Delicate cakes and pastries, painstakingly prepared, are a hallmark of Nonya cuisine. Specialities include vegetable-filled crisp pastry cases known as "top hats"; the spicy noodle dish of curry mee; a shaved ice and red bean dessert called *ice kacang*; and a variety of traditional cakes, or *kueh*, all rich in glutinous rice, coconut milk and palm sugar!

Left: Privacy and great views are assured at the exclusive Pangkor Laut Resort, located on a small island off the west coast of Perak.
Above, clockwise from top left: Scenes of some of Malaysia's top island resorts: the spa at Marina Bay Estates on Pangkor Laut island; an open-air bathroom in a sea villa at Pangkor Laut Resort; a living room at the Villa, the Andaman, on Langkawi Island; and a bedroom at the nearby resort, The Datai, also on Langkawi.

Left: Swimmers have the best of both worlds at Sarawak's Holiday Inn at Damai Beach, located on a beach near the mouth of the Santubong River and within easy reach of the award-winning Sarawak Cultural Village.

Right: As the largest resort complex in both Sabah and Malaysia, Sutera Harbour Resort boasts two five-star hotels, a country club, marina, extensive recreational facilities, and a host of restaurants to suit every taste.

Selected Further Reading

The Encyclopedia of Malaysia (Vol. 5): Architecture, Chen Voon Fee (editor), Archipelago Press, 1998

The Best of Borneo Travel, Victor T. King (compiler), Oxford University Press, 1992

The Complete Short Stories of W. Somerset Maugham, W. Somerset Maugham, Doubleday, 1953

The Crafts of Malaysia, Dato' Haji Sulaiman et al, Archipelago Press, 1994

East Malaysia and Brunei, Wendy Hutton (editor), Periplus Editions, 2nd edn 1997

Exciting Malaya: A Visual Journey, S. L. Wong, Periplus Editions, 1998

The Food of Malaysia: Authentic Recipes from the Crossroads of Asia, Periplus Editions, 1999

The Golden Chersonese and the Way Thither, Isabella L. Bird, 1883; reprinted Oxford University Press, 1980

Green Malaysia: Rainforst Encounters, Premilla Mohanlall, Malaysian Timber Council, 2002

A History of Malaysia, Barbara Watson Andaya and Leonard Y. Andaya, University of Hawaii Press, 2nd edn 2001

Into the Heart of Borneo, Redmond O'Hanlon, Salamander Press, 1984

The Long Day Wanes: A Malayan Trilogy (includes *Time for a Tiger* (1956), *The Enemy in the Blanket* (1958) and *Beds in the East* (1959)), Anthony Burgess, Norton, 1992

Malaysia: An Underwater Paradise, Andrea and Antonella Ferrari, Periplus Editions, 1998

Malaysian Journey, Rehman Rashid, Kuala Lumpur, 2nd edn 1993

They Came to Malaya: A Travellers' Anthology, J. M. Gullick (compiler), Oxford University Press, 1993

West Malaysia and Singapore, Wendy Moore (editor), Periplus Editions, 2nd edn 1998

The Soul of Malaya, Henri Fauconnier, 1931; reprinted Oxford University Press, 1990

Wild Malaysia: The Wildlife and Scenery of Peninsular Malaysia, Sarawak, and Sabah, Gerald Cubbitt and Junaidi Payne, Cambridge, MIT, 1991